Acknowledgements

International Poetry Review counts among its lifelong supporters the following poetry lovers:

Louis Bourne
Phil Cohen
Fred and Susan Chappell
Bernhard Frank
Alice Hill
Ruthie Katzenstein
Stevenson Lupton, Jr.
Karol Neufeld
David Schenck, Ph.D.
Maria H. Schilke
Dr. Alan E. Smith
David and Zita Smith
Mrs. Betty Watson

The *International Poetry Review* is published annually by the Department of Languages, Literatures, and Cultures at UNC Greensboro. The journal was previously published twice a year through Volume 42, Numbers 1 & 2 (Spring & Fall 2016).

Authors who would like to publish their work in English translation and translators who would like to publish their work, please email the editor, Rose Facchini, at rose.facchini@tufts.edu. Please do not send manuscripts by mail.

Annual subscriptions for individuals are available through the Department for $18. A $12 international shipping fee will be added for non-U.S. subscribers. To subscribe, call (336) 334-5655 or email amhontan@uncg.edu. Institutions can subscribe through EBSCO or other agencies for $22.

For product safety concerns under the European Union's General Product Safety Regulation (EU GPSR), please contact gpsr@mare-nostrum.co.uk or write to the University of North Carolina Press and Mare Nostrum Group B.V., Mauritskade 21D, 1091 GC Amsterdam, The Netherlands.

ISBN: 978-1-4696-9199-2

Cover image: © Chema Castelló, 2025.

Typesetting: Unmani Tewari

UNC
GREENSBORO
Department of
Languages, Literatures,
and Cultures

International Poetry Review

VOLUME 48 | 2025

EDITORS

Rose Facchini, Tufts U
Ana Hontanilla, UNC Greensboro

GUEST EDITOR FOR "MARK SMITH-SOTO: IT ALL MATTERS"

Mercer Bufter, UNC Greensboro

TRANSLATION EDITORS

Rose Facchini, Tufts U. Italian
Ana Hontanilla, UNC Greensboro. Spanish

POETRY READERS

Mercer Bufter, UNC Greensboro
Peter Dola, UNC Greensboro
Victor Pambuccian, Arizona State U

FOUNDING EDITOR

Evalyn Pierpoint Gill

WEBSITE MANAGER

Joshua Lunsford

Founded in 1975 by Evalyn Pierpoint Gill, *International Poetry Review* is dedicated to the idea that the world becomes a better place when we stop to explore and listen to the voices of writers in diverse languages and from different cultures. This journal published works by contemporary writers in all languages, with facing English translations. *International Poetry Review* is of interest to anyone who loves the rhythms and beauty of the written word in all languages.

Contents

8   Letter from the Editors

Dutch

12   **Anne Louïse van den Dool**, translated by Arno Bohlmeijer
"Vachtenwand" | "Fur Wall"

14   **Guillaume van der Graft**, translated by Arno Bohlmeijer
"Darlington"

16   **Ted van Lieshout**, translated by Arno Bohlmeijer
"Gespuis" | "Riffraff"

English

18   **Yuan Changming**, "Chinese Learning: Lesson 12"

19   **James Croal Jackson**, "What Will We Do with What Dad Kept?"

20   **David Dephy**, "The Waving Silk"

22   **Luke Dylan Ramsey**, "No Longer"

French

24   **Laura Hess**, translated by author
"Les merles bavardants" | "The Talkative Blackbirds"
"Les papillons légèrs" | "The Light Butterflies"

28　**Henri Meschonnic**, translated by Gaby Bedetti and Don Boes
Untitled ("nous répondons" | "we answer")

Italian
30　**Mirko Boncaldo**, translated by author
Untitled ("con le punta di dita" | "with the fingertips")
Untitled ("per ogni lacerto" | "for each barked")
Untitled ("Noi, rievocate rovine" | "We, evoked ruins by this fire")

36　**Antonio Spagnuolo**, translated by Ivano Mugnaini
"Ciclo" | "Cycle"
"Sorpresa" | "Surprise"
"Visione" | "Vision"

Portuguese
42　**Adriano Espínola**, translated by Charles Perrone
"Língua Mar" | "Sea-Language"
"A sumaúma" | "A Kapok Ceiba"
"O poeta chega aos 70" | "The Poet Makes It to Seventy"

Spanish
52　**Alberto Marcos**, , translated by Sacha Cooke
"Visita de obra" | "Site Visit"

52　**Jorge Armando Ríos**, translated by Ivy Raff
"In Memoriam: Antonio Deltoro"
"Es más probable" | "It's More Likely"

Special Features

58   Letter from the Guest Editor, "Mark Smith-Soto: It All Matters" by **Mercer Bufter**

65   Ten Poems from *Daybreak* by **Mark Smith-Soto** "Poetic License", "'So You Want to Be a Poet?'", "Tío", "Wonder", "Biography", "There You Are", "Café riff", "Beautiful", "Timely Gift", "Lost Poem"

76   Autobiography of Francesco Fazio, translated by Rose Facchini

78   Five Poems from *Risorgere dalle proprie ceneri* | *Rising from Ones's Ashes* by **Francesco Fazio** "Questo sconosciuto poeta" | "This Unknown Poet" "Frequenze in lotta" | "Wrestling Frequencies" "Quali dei due mondi?" | "Which of the Two Worlds?" "Alalà" "Il corpo-tempio" | "The Body-Temple"

91   **List of Contributors: Context Paragraphs and Biographies**

Letter from the Editors

In crafting this issue, a powerful and unifying theme emerged from the rich tapestry of poems: the exploration of contrasts within the broader lens of non-duality. Through the voices of poets from diverse backgrounds, this collection delves into the forces that define our lives—light and dark, resilience and surrender, reality and imagination. These poems thrive in the tension between life's most profound forces, inviting readers to reflect on moments of transformation and harmony that shape our existence. They explore deeply personal experiences, resonating with the complexities of human emotion and creating a mosaic of insights that speak to humanity's shared longing for renewal.

Non-duality, as a concept, transcends oppositions and instead delves into the interplay between contrasts and the non-dual unity they reveal. In poems like Guillaume van der Graft's "Darlington," the delicate interplay between loss and memory underscores how one shapes the other. Loss is not portrayed as an endpoint but as a transformative force, a prism through which memory is refracted, creating a nuanced perspective on what remains. Similarly, Ted van Lieshout's "Riffraff" presents resilience and surrender not as binary choices but as coexisting states of being. It invites readers to consider the courage required to persist and the vulnerability inherent in letting go, framing both as integral to the human experience. Luke Dylan Ramsey's "No Longer" brings another dimension to this theme through time's fleeting nature. The poem juxtaposes permanence and transience, reminding us that life's moments, though ephemeral, leave indelible imprints on the fabric of our existence.

Reality and its perception are intricately woven throughout this issue, blurring the boundaries between what is real and imagined. Francesco Fazio's "Which of the Two Worlds?" serves as a gateway into this exploration, likened to Alice in Wonderland's journey. It challenges readers to consider not just the worlds we inhabit but the ones we create within our minds. The surreal elements in Antonio Spagnuolo's "Cycle" deepen this exploration by presenting life as a series of transformations. His use of autobiographical loss becomes a metaphor for the larger human condition, illustrating how time can simultaneously oppress with its weight and liberate through renewal. Adriano Espínola's "The Poet Makes It to Seventy" offers a poignant reflection on the passage of time, portraying it as both a thief of youth and a giver of wisdom. The poet's nuanced portrayal of aging reframes duality not as opposition but as coexistence, where the burdens of age coexist with its gifts of resilience and insight.

In an age where technology often distances humanity from nature, several poems in this issue wrestle with the consequences of this disconnection. Fazio's "The Body-Temple" juxtaposes the relentless noise of modern life with the grounding rhythms of the Earth, presenting a stark contrast that underscores the urgency of reconnection. This dichotomy is echoed in Ramsey's "No Longer," which frames humanity's awakening to Earth's rhythms as both a deeply personal and collective act. Alberto Marcos' "Site Visit" and Fazio's "Alalà" pivot towards moments of clarity and renewal, offering a hopeful vision of rediscovery amidst chaos. These poems do not merely lament the alienation of humanity from nature; they act as invitations to reimagine a harmonious relationship, urging readers to listen to the Earth's quiet wisdom.

The poems in this issue masterfully explore the entwined forces of destruction and liberation. Fazio's "Wrestling Frequencies" uses the metaphor of a battle to represent the internal struggle to preserve one's essence in a chaotic world. The poem captures the tension between succumbing to external pressures and reclaiming inner freedom, resonating as a universal struggle. Mirko Boncaldo's untitled piece with the haunting line "We, evoked ruins by this fire" amplifies this theme with vivid imagery of fire consuming and transforming. Here, destruction is not an end but a necessary precursor to liberation—a rebirth from the ashes. These poems challenge readers to see beyond the immediate devastation, to the potential for renewal and growth that lies within it.

Despite the diversity of themes and voices, the collection weaves a cohesive narrative that reflects the shared complexities of the human condition. Van der Graft's "Darlington" and Spagnuolo's "Cycle" are prime examples of how deeply personal experiences resonate universally. The exploration of loss, renewal, and self-discovery in these works invites readers to find echoes of their own journeys, fostering a profound connection between poet and audience. This issue becomes a mirror, reflecting not just individual experiences but the shared emotions, struggles, aspirations, and existential questions that define the human expierience.

The shattered mirror on the cover page serves as a visual encapsulation of the themes explored in this issue. Each share, reflecting a different scene, symbolizes the fragmented nature of perception and the multiplicity of truths that coexist within any experience. The blooming flowers evoke renewal and beauty, while the empty urban street suggests isolation and alienation. The ethereal glow hints at transcendence, reminding readers of the elusive and transformative power of poetry. These shards, though fragmented, come together to form a cohesive whole, much like the poems in this issue. Each piece contributes to a broader narrative of human fragility and strength, inviting us to embrace the tensions and dualities of life with courage and grace.

In this issue, readers will find two special dossiers. The first is an in-memoriam tribute to Mark Smith-Soto, honoring his legacy and lasting impact on the literary community. Smith-Soto served as editor of *International Poetry Review* from 1992 to 2014, but even after stepping down, he remained a guiding presence, offering support, insights, and encouragement until his passing in 2023. His dedication to poetry and his unwavering commitment to this publication continue to inspire. The second dossier features a selection of poems by Francesco Fazio, whose work resonates deeply with the themes explored in this issue. We hope that these poems inspire you to pause, reflect, and rediscover the connections between your inner world and the rhythms that bind us all.

Rose Facchini, Tufts University

Ana Hontanilla, University of North Carolina Greensboro

"Vachtenwand"

Anne Louïse van den Dool

Soms hoop ik dat je verdwijnt
op een manier die mij geen pijn doet:
schelpen die je stilletjes in hun huizen zuigen
tijdens een wandeling op het strand
of hoe je na een korte val van een klimwand
door de kussenvloer wordt opgenomen.

Ik zal daar dan alleen staan
en weten dat ik me dit over je heb afgevraagd:
vier zachte vachtenwanden die als in een liftschacht
me steeds dichter bleven naderen,
als die keer dat we een te klein woonmuseum
met te veel mooie spullen bezochten,
alles blonk, alles glom,
alles een geur, alles een motief,

en jij zei:
zoveel schoons,
ik wil hier weg.

"Fur Wall"

Anne Louïse van den Dool, translated by Arno Bohlmeijer

Sometimes I hope you'll vanish
in a manner that won't hurt me:
shells that quietly suck you inside
during a walk on the beach,
or the way you're being drawn into the pad-floor
after a short fall from a climbing wall.

I'll be left by myself,
knowing what I've thought-brought upon you:
four soft fur walls that kept coming closer
like an elevator shaft,
or when we were in a too small house-museum
with too many beautiful things,
all were shining and all gleamed,
everything a smell, everywhere designs,

and you said:
all so fine, all so clean,
I'm out of here.

"Darlington"

Guillaume van der Graft

Vijf is Renee. Ze gelooft in kabouters.
Ze stuurt mij een briefkaart omdat ik op reis ben.
Ze ruimde de bladeren in de tuin.

Wanneer de winter voorbij is, de zomer
gekomen als tweemaal twee is vier
wie zal haar verzekeren dat wij leven?

Wij worden niet ouder dan kabouters.
Wij sterven zo ongemerkt als dwergen
aan bomen van kennis, een volk vol ernst.

De tijd weet van neits

Oud worden is niet moeilijk,
het is onmogelijk, men blijft

het nadenkende kind, de popelende
minnaar, de man, de beschaamde vader,

maar steeds meer afgedane tijd begraaft zich
in huid en lijf en leden tot

alles is eengeworden met de dagen
die zijn voorbijgegaan. Men sterft vanzelf.

"Darlington"

Guillaume van der Graft, translated by Arno Bohlmeijer

She's five, Renee. She believes in gnomes.
As I'm traveling, she sends me a postcard.
She cleared the leaves in the yard.

When the winter is over, the summer
has come like two and two make four,
who will assure her that we're living?

We don't grow older than gnomes.
We die as unnoticed as little creatures
on trees of knowledge, a serious people indeed.

TIME IS INNOCENT, DOESN'T KNOW

Growing old isn't difficult,
it's impossible, one remains

the pensive child, the craving
lover, the man, the father ashamed,

but more and more finished time lays
in skin and flesh and limbs until

all is united with the days
that passed by. Dying is a fact of life.

"Gespuis"

Ted van Lieshout

Ik zou niet willen denken aan de dood.
Maar met elke stap die ik zet vermorzel
ik diertjes die ik niet zie of herken.

Ik moet ook leven met Karel die wormen
de kop afbijt en Daan die spinnen minder
dan acht poten gunt en ik geef toe:

ik kluif het laatste stukje kip van bot.
Kan ik nog dieper vallen? Kan er niet
een kikker komen die ik dapper kus?

"Riffraff"

Ted van Lieshout, translated by Arno Bohlmeijer

I'd rather not think of death.
But with every step, I'm crushing
little creatures I don't see or recognize.

I also need to live with Charlie, who bites
the heads off worms, and Dan, who grants
a spider less than eight legs, and I admit:

I dig into the last bit of chicken.
Can I sink any lower? Won't a frog
show up that I'll boldly give a snog?

"Chinese Learning: Lesson 12"

Yuan Changming

Square-shaped, stroke-structured
Every Chinese character presents an
Abstract painting rich in symbolic
Meanings; for example, '自由'
[Freedom] is an enclosed framework
Where there's always a unique stroke
Trying to break out of the cell
Whereas '牢笼' [prison house] is
Open-ended in every direction, but
Even if you are as strong as a bull
Or a dragon, you can never hope to
Escape from under a simple radical

"What Will We Do with What Dad Kept?"

James Croal Jackson

       Frisbee thrown by my brother at
our mother's home, rising with wind–
           he asks a question I can't catch.

"The Waving Silk"

David Dephy

If only I could find
the way in the night,
I would be almighty.

There are the seconds
when I am aware
of your distant beauty,

far beyond my existence,
and seconds when I am not.
I want you to know that my heart

beats by your breath—
the silk softly waves
by the breeze every morning,

and that song, sound from my childhood,
sound of hope and magnets is playing
in my mind when I feel your lights at night,

some familiar voice echoes
from the other side of alone.
If only I could let go of emptiness,

I would be the waving silk.
Hey dear friend,
with distant heavenly eyes,

this night is calling me again.
To understand you maybe is to be
like you, but to love you

is to be the waving silk
appearing after awakening
by the breeze every morning.

"No Longer"

Luke Dylan Ramsey

though it was medicinal
I quit the weed quit the drinking
stopped drugging myself
I am lucid now, but the past...
hangs around me hidden behind
all that I see even the sky above
clouds spell out your name
your face is the moon
your brain its dark side

we got lucky at the border crossing
your son always told on me
my body fluids forever revealed my secrets

I burned the paintings deleted the evidence
there's nothing of you left inside here
tap tap tapping my chest
still everywhere is where I see you
you're the linkage the fruit the berries

I love a tangent
I love to digress

"Les merles bavardants"

Laura Hess

J'allais partout enveloppée des merles.
Ils formaient un nuage autour de moi.
Ma mère ne me voyait plus—elle voyais
les merles et elle entendait leur chanson
au lieu de ma voix qui est devenue noire
à cause de tous ces merles chantant quand
j'ouvrais la bouche. O, mère, écoutez!
Je suis dans le nuage de ces merles toujours.
Je suis où vous m'avez laissée, quand le ciel
est ouvert et vous m'avez dit de me taire.

"The Talkative Blackbirds"

Laura Hess, translated by author

I went everywhere surrounded by blackbirds.
They formed a cloud around me.
My mother saw me no more—she saw
the blackbirds and she heard their song
instead of my voice which became black
as a result of all those blackbirds singing when
I opened my mouth. O, mother, listen!
I am always in a cloud of these blackbirds.
I am where you left me, when the sky
opened and you told me to shut up.

"Les papillons légèrs"

Laura Hess

J'allais partout entourée d'un nuage de papillons.
Leurs ailes me touchaient légèrement
comme si pour dire—tu n'es guère ici.
Et en vérité, je suis devenue presque perdue
dans mes pensées, mes pensées de voler.
Comme autrefois je pouvais le faire,
voler vite mais en effet près de la terre.
Au lieu de voler, maintenant je reste très immobile
ayant été élevé dans un nuage de papillons
vers un monde où voler c'est respirer
et où vous, mon cheri, ne me touchez plus.

"The Light Butterflies"

Laura Hess, translated by author

I went everywhere surrounded by a cloud of butterflies.
Their wings touched me lightly
as if to say—*you are hardly here.*
And in truth, I became almost lost
in my thoughts, my thoughts of flying.
As I used to be able to fly,
fly fast but in fact close to the earth.
Instead of flying, now I stay still
having been raised in a cloud of butterflies
into a world where to fly is to breathe
and where you, my dear, do not touch me anymore.

Untitled

Henri Meschonnic

nous répondons
ne sachant pas si la question pour laquelle nous sommes debout
vient des années passées ou de celles
que nous ne connaissons pas
le pain la table sont les témoins
qui signent aujourd'hui
parce que nous tournons dans le visage l'un de l'autre
comme l'abeille et la fleur
et que l'espace autour de nous
répond même
avant la question

Untitled

Henri Meschonnic, translated by Gaby Bedetti and Don Boes

we answer
not knowing whether the question we are facing
comes from years past
or years we've lost
the bread the table are the witnesses
that mark the day
because we turn toward each other
like the bee and the flower
and the space around us
provides an answer even
before the question

Untitled

Mirko Boncaldo

con le punta di dita, rorida
come brina sulle sgretolate screpolature
vieni
e sobilli atavici sedimenti
di fiori sconosciuti e incandescenti
incredule ombre
che l'acqua non regna, lontana
che banga:

suffragetta, partigiana, *femme*

Untitled

Mirko Boncaldo, translated by author

with the fingertips, dewy
on the crumbled cracks
comes
and arouse atavistic sediments
of unknown flowers and incandescent
incredulous shades
that water doesn't reign, far away
that wets:

suffragette, partisan, *femme.*

Untitled

Mirko Boncaldo

per ogni lacerto latrato
che la storia non racconta
raccolgo ogni memoria

è la scorta di scarti accumulata
rimossa
blinde
che più non si dice.

scancellata
logorata
massacrata

è l'ultima non l'ultima rivolta parola
quella che si perde
quella che non si ritrova.
apolide

Untitled

Mirko Boncaldo, translated by author

for each barked fragment
that the story does not tell
I collect every memory.

is the accumulated scrap stock
removed
blinded
which is no longer said.

erased
worn out
massacred

it is the last not the last told word
the one that is lost
the one that is not found.
displaced.

Untitled

Mirko Boncaldo

Noi, rievocate rovine da questo fuoco
come tribù danziamo
più estranei di astri
senza pudore.
Noi là, alla Pecoramorta, le estati
nelle turpitudini sabbie immergiamo
per masticarci la notte
rosse gonfie lune.
Noi che ai denti opponiamo le lingue
e ci trafughiamo negli indumenti.
Noi abbiamo il senso
dell'irruzione,
impeto d'una liberazione,
Noi, noi che non sapevamo come vivere
che volevamo essere vissuti.

Untitled

Mirko Boncaldo, translated by author

We, evoked ruins by this fire
as a tribe we dance
stranger than shameless stars.
We there, at Deadsheep, the summers
in the turpitude sands we immerse ourselves
to chew the night away
swollen red moons.
We who oppose our tongues to our teeth
and steal ourselves into our clothes.
We have the sense
of the irruption,
impetus for liberation.
We, we who didn't know how to live,
who wanted to be lived.

"Ciclo"

Antonio Spagnuolo

Ho terminato il mio ciclo!
Lascio un segno nell'ultima pagina
a sigillo del tempo perduto
e del balzo saltato fuori dall'incognita.
Vorrei chiuderla qui, nella penombra
di una sera piovigginosa
per spezzare finalmente le spranghe
che mi vennero addosso.
Eppure hai ceduto nel momento della debolezza
alle suggestioni dei richiami
di una plenitudine che inganna.

"Cycle"

Antonio Spagnuolo, translated by Ivano Mugnaini

I have finished my cycle!
I leave a checkmark on the last page
to seal the lost time
and the spark jumped out of the incognita.
I would like to close it here, in the dim light
of a drizzling evening
to finally break the bars
that came upon me.
Yet you surrendered in the moment of weakness
to the allurements of the calling voice
of a deceiving crowd.

"Sorpresa"

Antonio Spagnuolo

Nella sorpresa riordino il conforto
della tua parola,
mi vieni al fianco nell'ombra
fingendo una presenza che svanisce
nell'incerto palpeggio dei colori.
Una violenza che ha segnato l'addio
quando tentai di confondere minacce
esplose nell'inganno.
Non basterà la brace a sospendere
la dolcezza che consumava silenzi
e delicatamente insinuava abbandoni.

"Surprise"

Antonio Spagnuolo, translated by Ivano Mugnaini

By surprise I recollect the comfort
of your word,
while you come to my side in the shadows
simulating a presence that fades away
in the uncertain touch of colors.
That same violence marked the farewell
when I tried to confuse the threats
blown up by the deception.
The embers will not be enough to wipe away
the sweetness that consumed silences
and gently predicted abandonment.

"Visione"

Antonio Spagnuolo

Inutile giostra il susseguirsi
dei giorni ora che il tempo srotola
le ore nel ritmo incalzante del minuto,
che insegue ingenuamente le intensità
cangianti.
Il dono inatteso nella stanza che imbruna,
fuori dal rituale, esita a un balzo,
ancora nel tormento crede agli estremi.
Urlando l'incubo della vendetta
non sono che placenta segreta
nei frammenti di una visione.

"Vision"

Antonio Spagnuolo, translated by Ivano Mugnaini

The sequence of the days is a useless
carousel now that time unrolls the hours
in the unrelenting rhythm
of the minute, naively chasing
iridescent intensities.
The unexpected gift in the darkening room,
outside the ritual, hesitates to dare a leap,
hurt by anguish it still believes in the extremes.
Screaming the nightmare of vengeance
I am just a secret placenta
in the fragments of a vision.

"Língua Mar"

Adriano Espínola

A língua em que navego, marinheiro,
na proa das vogais e consoantes,
é a que me chega em ondas incessantes
à praia deste poema aventureiro.
É a língua portuguesa, a que primeiro
transpôs o abismo e as dores velejantes,
no mistério das águas mais distantes,
e que agora me banha por inteiro.
Língua de sol, espuma e maresia,
que a nau dos sonhadores-navegantes
atravessa a caminho dos instantes,
cruzando o Bojador de cada dia.
Ó língua-mar, viajando em todos nós.
No teu sal, singra errante a minha voz.

"Sea-Language"

Adriano Espínola, translated by Charles Perrone

The tongue on which I sail— seafaring men—
in consonants and vowels proclaimed on prow,
the one that flows to me in waves that plough,
this venturesome poem at sandy den,
is Portuguese, the first to pass with ken
abyss and pain that's worn on sailors' brow,
and mystery of waters far somehow,
now bathing me entirely again.
A language of ocean's sun, smell and foam
that ships of dreams and navigators vow
to cross and search to find a timely now,
Cape Bojador traversed on daily roam.
Oh yes, sea-tongue, a voyage of our choice,
in all your salt does sail adrift my voice.

"A sumaúma"

Adriano Espínola

No alto amazonas
entre matas densas
a sumaúma assoma.

Raízes tabulares
imensas feito uma
harpa de cordas tensas

se lançam aos pares.
O poeta disfarçado
de curupira bate

nelas os calcanhares
pra fazer ressoar de
perto a melodia

clarescura da tarde
o lamento da terra
e a vertigem dos ares

quando lá nas alturas
ruge a tempestade
e no chão a motosserra.

"A Kapok Ceiba"

Adriano Espínola, translated by Charles Perrone

In the upper Amazon
in vegetation so dense
the silk-cotton tree's on.

Roots tabular flare
as immense as harps with
their strings taut and tense

shooting out in pairs.
Disguised as a bogeyman
the poet now strikes them

with his heels held square
to bring close the sound
of chiaroscuro melody

in the afternoon found
the lament of the earth and
the vertiginous air

when up there on high
the storm can't but roar
as chainsaws on the ground.

"O poeta chega aos 70"

Adriano Espínola

Como quem não quer nada,
dobro a esquina
um pouco mais inclinada
dos 70.

(Festa de lobos,
de loucos anos
passados em surdina).

Alguém logo se aproxima
e no meu peito cola;
um outro de mim
se desprende e cala.

Quem são, indago,
o corpo rente
ao branco muro em frente,
que me dividem
assim em dois,
entre o sonho do que fui
e a vigília imprevisível
do depois?

Agora, sei:
olá sombras amigas,
vinde clarear
as minhas têmporas
antigas
e os gestos e os sinais
que emito de passagem!

"The Poet Makes It to Seventy"

Adriano Espínola, translated by Charles Perrone

Somewhat nonchalantly
do I turn the corner,
a bit more inclined,
of 70.

(Feast of wild wolves,
of crazy years gone by
spent quietly on the sly).

Someone soon draws closer
and presses on my chest;
an other from me
comes loose to stay silent.

Who are they, I inquire,
my body right next
to the blank wall and spire,
who divide me
thusly in two,
between dreams of what I was and
the unforeseeable awakened state
of what comes later?

And now I know:
old friends' shades, hello!
do come light up
my ancient
temples
and the gestures and signals
that I emit in passage!

Exclamo, expectante,
sem mágoa nem nostalgia,
ao chegar a salvo
da pandemia
e dessa viagem no tempo,
náufrago de amores
e fracassos,
à beira do cais
dos meus próprios passos.

Quem, pergunto a elas,
me inventa
a cada instante
a cada dia
ao dobrar a esquina
dos 70?

Uma sombra obstinada
súbito avança e me ilumina.
E é Ninguém.
E é Ulisses com a espada.
Martim Soares Moreno e Araquém,
combatendo em uma praia
do passado, mais além.

Lâminas, lendas e lutas
pretéritas
(que me pertencem também)
me atravessam,
junto a esse muro
rabiscado do presente,
memória do futuro.

I exclaim, expectant,
without nostalgia or grief,
upon safe arrival
from the pandemic
and this voyage through time,
castaway from love
and failures,
by the dock and reef
of my own step-filled mime.

Who, I go on to ask them,
invents me
every second
each and every day
upon turning the corner
of 70?

A sudden shade obstinately
comes forward to illuminate me.
And it is Nobody.
And it's Odysseus with his sword.
Portuguese explorer and native shaman
in combat on a beach
in the past, beyond reach.

Steel, stories, and struggles
in the preterite
(that belong to me as well)
now traversing me,
there by that wall
with the present's flat scrawl,
memory of the future.

E já sou eu agora
que sou nada,
triste animal de tão contente,
tecedor da arte dos enganos
(que é a poesia,
essa estranha arte
pródiga de espantos),
feito um cego
numa calçada,
tocando à parte,
por onde passo
e para onde sempre vou.

E chego
por descuido de algum
travesso arcano
à esquina
desses inesperados anos,
sendo o que sou:
um homem comum,
carne e terra girantes
do acaso,
70 vezes em um.

And now I'm already myself,
I who am naught,
sad creature so content,
weaver of the art of deceit
(that is poetry,
that strangest of arts
of prodigal amazements),
like a blind man
on a sidewalk,
touching aside apart,
where I am passing by
and where I shall always go.

And I arrive
by dint of some
arcane mischief
at the corner of
these unexpected years,
being what I am:
a common man,
spinning flesh and earth
of fateful chance,
70 times in one.

"Visita de obra"

Alberto Marcos

No soy yo quien atraviesa
estos valles prendidos de ocres,
ni este el tren que me lleva
de un lugar a otro lugar.

La tierra se retuerce
mostrando sus costuras
y de las balsas de agua
emana un vapor sin voz.

Los túneles construyen el paisaje
con su lenguaje de fronteras.

En el vidrio reflejado,
superpuesto a los adolescentes chopos,
a los desnudos almendros de otoño,
a las hayas, sabinas y retama,
al maíz con sus artríticos penachos secos,
mi rostro descansa entre los otros.

Por delante del dormido campanario,
de la vejiga de la fábrica,
de los afilados dedos de los álamos,
otros ensayan a escuchar
el rumor de un tren que nunca se detiene.

"Site Visit"

Alberto Marcos, translated by Sacha Cooke

It is not I who traverses
these valleys hung in ochres,
nor this the train that takes me
from one place to another.

The earth writhes
uncovering its seams,
and from the water reservoirs
a voiceless vapor rises.

Tunnels build the landscape up
with their language of borders.

Reflected on the glass,
superimposed over the adolescent black poplars,
the naked almond trees of autumn,
the beeches, Phoenician junipers and brooms,
the cornfields with their arthritic dry cobs,
my face rests amongst the others.

In front of the sleeping bell tower,
the factory's bladder,
and the sharpened fingers of the poplars,
others are rehearsing to listen
to the whisper of this train that never stops.

"In Memoriam: Antonio Deltoro"

Jorge Armando Ríos

«Tú no lo conociste», me dijeron
como al que llegó muy tarde,
y ése es un dolor que aporto al final de la hilera.
Pero sí lo conocí
cuando nos leía
desde una barranca más abajo,
su voz mineral
cruzando del altavoz
hacia el martes y los árboles,
tendiendo versos cual puentes
que retumban todavía

"In Memoriam: Antonio Deltoro"

Jorge Armando Ríos, translated by Ivy Raff

You didn't know him, they said,
as if to someone who'd arrived late in evening,
& this pain I will carry to the end of the line.
But I did know him
when he read to us
from a deep ravine,
his mineral voice
crossing the speaker
toward Tuesday & the trees,
laying verses like bridges
that still rumble

"Es más probable"

Jorge Armando Ríos

morir
camino al aeropuerto
que en un avión;
morir haciendo un caldo
que en un avión;
en un accidente con el cepillo dental
o al cambiar una bombilla;
morir por una alimaña en la cama,
o ahogado con un cacahuate.
Resulta que es más probable morir
no volando,
sino ahorita
cuando se es
ordinario y corriente.

"It's More Likely"

Jorge Armando Ríos, translated by Ivy Raff

you'll die
on the way to the airport
than on the plane

you'll die making soup
than on a plane

you'll die
in an accident with a toothbrush
or changing a light bulb

you'll die by a spider in bed
or choked by a peanut

> it turns out it's more likely you'll die
> not while flying,
> but right now
> while ordinary

The author and translator felt that this change in stanzas and indentation
best captures the spirit of the poem.

Mark Smith-Soto: It All Matters

"We must tend our garden." –Voltaire

Mark Smith-Soto served as editor of *International Poetry Review* from 1992 until 2014. His first appearance in the journal was in the spring of 1990, as both a translator and guest editor. That issue featured a dossier showcasing the work of twenty-six South American women writers, curated by Ramiro Lagos, an associate editor of the journal at the time and a close friend and mentor to Mark. Even after stepping down as editor, Mark continued to offer guidance, suggestions, and support to the publication until his death in 2023.

Mark's approach to writers modeled the treatment he wanted to receive when he himself submitted his own work for publication. He engaged with poems with sincerity and curiosity, striving to uncover their essence and always addressing writers with respect. Although he had a deep love for rhymed poetry and grew up memorizing poems, Mark remained open to free verse and more contemporary poetic forms. He actively sought diverse perspectives, inviting writers with varied backgrounds to serve as readers for the magazine's English-language submissions (I was one of them for a time). He encouraged lively—and sometimes "lawyerly"—debates about a poem's meaning and whether it truly had something to say.

He approached his editorial work with both rigor and optimism, firmly believing that every new submission held the potential for extraordinary translations or beautiful poetry. I had the privilege of working with him on a few issues near the end of his tenure as editor. During editorial sessions, he could be persuaded, but only if you truly understood the poem you were advocating for. Like all true artists, Mark had a clear sense of what he liked while remaining committed to pushing his own boundaries. He wanted to understand new styles of writing, and he was always ready to welcome another beautiful work of art into his experience.

In his poetry, Mark wrote with clarity and transparency, aiming for his words to resonate and be understood by as many people as possible. He deliberately crafted resonant stories at the heart of each poem, a process he once described to me with care. Over more than a decade, we met regularly to exchange poems, critique each other's work, and, in the process, attempt to solve the world's problems through dialogue.

I met Mark while I was completing a master's degree at the University of North Carolina Greensboro. I had moved to Greensboro a few years earlier, following my MFA in Poetry from New York University. Between raising a young family and managing the demands of my studies, I hadn't written a poem in years.

A mutual friend introduced us, and we met at Tate Street Coffee House. Sitting at the window table, his inquisitive, lawyer-like eyebrow arched up and down as we shared poems for the first time. We quickly became close friends, and in the coming years, I would often hear his voice cutting across the café as he recited A.E. Housman or W.B. Yeats, Francisco de Quevedo or Manuel Gutiérrez Nájera.

A dozen years later, we sat in his sunroom, a space that often found its way into his "meditation" poems, and discussed his latest revision. It was a poem I'd seen years before. He'd refined the grace notes of the final image, swerved at the ending, and delivered the emotional punch that he wanted.

Over the years, I witnessed many of Mark's poems dive deep and resurface, transformed. He'd done it again. Less than two months later, by the end of October, he was gone.

***

One Sunday, Mark and I sat at the café. During a lull in our conversation, our minds wandered to separate places, and Mark's eyes roamed the crowd. After a moment, he shook his head, then began speaking with quiet intensity about a young man, a true artist, who had died believing he didn't matter. It took me a minute to catch on: Mark was mourning the death, as if it had just happened, of John Keats and the bitter irony of his epitaph: "Here lies One Whose Name was writ in Water."

When I think about that moment today, it accords perfectly with Mark's own poetry. "Meaning" and "mattering" are two watchwords of his work, and it was crucial to him that his poetry could be understood by anyone, regardless of their background in literature. His experience with the Men's Movement sparked this, he told me. While attending a large conference, he saw men who probably thought they didn't care about poetry moved to tears as they listened to poems: open, vulnerable, finding meaning. Mark always imagined his work speaking directly to a real audience of real people.

"It matters, Merc," he'd say to me, whether describing a chance encounter with an old friend, relating a memory of a family member, or recounting a story from the news. In addition to his "meditations," he often wrote poetry that responded to real-world events, calling the most emotionally gorged of these his "moral sharpies." Cruelty outraged him, bigotry outraged him, and poetry was one of his ways to fight back.

In many cases, we're forced to admit, as Mark once said to me, "The art is wiser than the artist." Not every brilliant artist is automatically a wise or compassionate person. With Mark, we have both. From his undying love for his wife, Beth (*ayer, hoy, y siempre*); to his "Little Brother" from the Big Brothers program, Manuel; to the siblings, cousins, and other family members he cherished both in daily life and in verse, Mark's wisdom on the page grew out of the wisdom he earned through empathy, struggle, and hard work throughout his life.

Like any great poet, Mark's work spanned a wide range of concerns. He wrote about his experiences as an overweight misfit arriving in the United States, he wrote about discrimination and racism, he wrote about culture shock. He wrote about marriage and aging, he wrote about nature and memory. Over the course of his career, he published literary criticism, translations, chapbooks, and full volumes. The opening lines of his poem "Wonder," from *Daybreak* (2024), could serve as a mission statement for a key aspect of his work:

Imperative: to make a space for wonder
in the self. I.e., stare hard at a pebble
until it trembles with a bit of thunder.

To me, his most characteristic poems are the "fourteeners": the sonnets and near-sonnets. These poems build in intensity, gaining momentum until they strike the reader as a complete whole. They present situations rather than collections of well-crafted images or observations. They are almost better summarized than quoted a line or two at a time:

The artistic boy whose father gently teases him about living in a "garrett."
The uncle, his secret not yet revealed, reciting poems in a speeding Opel.
The unsettling voices through the first telephones in Costa Rica.
The cost of innocent wonder as a glass picture window kills a bird in flight.
The man still in pain, still bewildered by a loved one's suicide, decades later.

In much of his best work, those stories also bring forward complex, unforgettable images. In "The tree my mother saved," the ordinary act of pruning a tree becomes something more: a timeless sculpture. At the same time, the emotions tied to the event reverse their opposites:

ruthlessness assumes the guise of care; the hard-earned salvation of the tree is deflated at the last moment. It only outlived its pruner by two years. The poem pulls in two directions simultaneously, never telling the reader how to feel about that tension.

The tree my mother saved by ruthlessly
cutting back the flowing, overextended limbs,
Venus de Milo of our front garden, still
impressive in its abbreviated gestures,
outlived her by two years only.

In "Mate," the poet seems to retell the story (a true one) of beating a chess legend in an exhibition match. However, in the last line, a different narrative is revealed. The poem begins: "I beat Bobby Fischer, he was playing sixty / people at the same time and I was fourteen." The last lines change everything:

not bad my father said on the way home.

The moment of emotion takes the reader by surprise. The poem suddenly shifts to being about a father and son, conveyed in the most understated way. The entire interaction is delivered in one breath, hurried and unbroken, without quotation marks or pauses.

In "Satori," Mark describes the slow awakening to the discovery of a beloved woman moving around (what must be) his kitchen, "wearing / what must be my red shirt." He watches her as though he himself is not there. His life comes into focus:

it comes to me then that I have
wandered in my life from dream to dream,
with a lotus of awakening about to open.

***

By the time I met him, he had already endured his major battle with cancer, and modern medicine was keeping it at bay. Maybe that's one reason his poems are so focused on time. Mark knew his time was finite. "I know it's true, I'm never going again to Paris, that time has blinked away," he wrote in "Timely Gift." In his beautiful, classical poem "Segue," he finds "death" inescapable, both in its rhymes and its stark banality:

Now that you mention it: death,
the cherry outside the kitchen
in full bloom, the novel I left
open on my bed ...

But his poetry is not morbid, and his interest in time is not driven by melancholy. We often discussed how much a person can change from their youth to early adulthood to old age, and what a wonderful thing that is. This is the explicit concern of *Berkeley Prelude* (2012), a long poem in eight movements. In this volume, the poet reflects on the young man he once was in the third person, commenting on these remembered scenes from the perspective of a wiser present.

The inspiration of the book is, of course, Wordsworth. "I was the Dreamer, they the Dream; I roamed / Delighted through the motley spectacle." Using those lines as an epigram, Mark explores the exhilarations, confusions, desires, and irreversible regrets that come into life like sudden weather. He also directly describes the work of the poet reclaiming them.

How to reweave that cloth...
                              ... tapping away
at a laptop in a crowded college coffeehouse
with chatter and young laughter all around,
while the sense of what's been lost and gained
pools in thoughts that lie too deep for tears.

When he died, Mark was in the process of completing his final book, *Daybreak*. When I told friends about him, I'd say, "He's a septuagenarian poet who hustles like he's twenty-five!" He was always rewriting, always submitting poems, and never getting used to editors' rejections.

"Have I shown you this email, Merc? You're not going to believe it." Then he would read the questionable rejection email aloud, the words booming through the café.

In Mark's poems, flashpoints of emotion never grow cold: some pangs of regret, love, grief, and wonder feel brand new every time you encounter them. These powerful emotions sprout and regenerate in your garden, as long as you continue to tend it.

A few years before he died, Mark began recommending *Candide* to me. "We must tend our garden," he would say. It was a happy confluence of life and art, because Mark himself had taken to his garden quite literally, planting flowers and cultivating spaces for birds.

Mark's blend of a well-examined life and a canon of poems known by heart allowed him to create a rich garden. He did the weeding, pruning, and nurturing of shoots necessary to live empathetically and to create with boldness as a writer, editor, and man.

Ten Poems from *Daybreak* by Mark Smith-Soto

"Poetic License"

I make free with my brothers in my dreams,
chortling from miles and lives away, years
and tears away, conjuring metaphors winsome
with mango trees, papayas and Lorca guitars,

memorious tweaks at every turn. I exile them
barefoot, bronze-cheeked from the Costa Rica
beaches where coconut palms nodded solemn
over their dreams and into American brick

boxes where their guardian angels left them
in the care of school patrols at crosswalks, astray
in gringo land. But how those boys branched

and bloomed in the strange new light! How they
chuckle and jeer, now, to find themselves launched
into yet another of my goddam poems.

"So You Want To Be A Poet?"

What was a garret? My dad spelled it out:
poets survived in them as best they could,
fed their art with their hunger, went without.
Not a trade I was eager for, just a kid

smitten with Lorca and Darío, dumbstruck
in a new land, a chub who doted on grilled
cheese with chips, peanut-brittle crunch.
No martyr in the name of art, me. Still,

still, could a garret be worse than where I
maundered, so-called Glass Manor, grey mortar,
grey brick? And the growl of *garret* in my
throat was an age-old call to arms: no comfort

foods could match the thrill of honoring,
with its rightful name, some humble thing.

"Tío"

Turns out you were not pure, turns out you were not good.
In the green Opel bound for Puntarenas, Pop a frown and silence
at the wheel, you whistled Beethoven to cheer the air, a sound
I took for your soul, lithe, handsome, free. Three kids huddled

and joyful in the dented coupe, we clamored for more of
the poems you recited like they might make life matter. For me,
you were everything that meant Uncle. Sometimes, you'd sigh
from the empty place where you kept the son you cheated,

the wife you cheated on, the loneliness I was to understand
too well. A vacation from yourself those long trips were,
the self you spared us, the details alien and banal, the loss
they brought. The singing light gutters under all that truth—

but holds you still, turning to face us from the front seat of the Opel
to recite the first poetry of our lives, your every fault forgiven.

"Wonder"

Imperative: to make a space for wonder
in the self. I.e., stare hard at a pebble
until it trembles with a bit of thunder,
the mere fact of its being. The trouble

is not fooling myself about it, just
because I want it so. A rust-limned petal
that lights from the dogwood on my wrist,
a leaf that cracks the argument of metal

gutters—these. But, say, a peony? It doesn't
count, does it? perfume and size to fill
any sentimental eye with quotidian awe.

It's about small, humble things . . . But mustn't
be facile, my abiding sin: What's colorful
or big, may be awesome . . . If only one saw.

"Biography"

When did he begin to think of himself
in the third person? Did he divide in
two when the propeller plane peeled off
from the tiny Alajuela airport, him cradling

his face in his arms, his kidnapped mind
blanking what it couldn't unsee. Maybe
it was later, when mamacita left him behind
to go back to her father's dying—painful to say

even now: *la muerte de mi abuelito.*
The split might run even deeper, to the maid
I loved who rocked me like a mother might,
or later when *limonada* became lemonade.

Or just some too perfect day, one like this,
stopped at a life . . . not just mine, not just his.

"There You Are"

I do feel somehow exiled here, outside
the frame— just what is it about a woman
at an open window, seen from the side,
an opalescent half light on her hands

holding the curtains apart, head tilted,
questioning? Maybe her gaze has stranded
on that naked lady half-hidden by the shed,
a blossom she knows she never planted,

her wondering, *These small, random gifts,*
why do they touch one so? But of course,
I can't begin to guess her mind, it's

me trespassing here, I should go before
she sees me, leave her to her thoughts—
"Oh, there you are, *amor.* Come look at this."

"Café Riff"

The fashions of my Berkeley youth, rounding
back—sweet ebb and flow of pot, the barista
in a tie-dye top, thin guys with scruffy beards.

Satchmo, timeless then and now, wheezes, rasps,
sails above it all, the college voices arguing,
loud clatter of all sorts minus the stitch

of laughter. Maybe not much to joke about
of late? Politics and outrage are in again,
like us back in the day, when we were grand—

dour, indignant, bell-bottomed, high-geared.
No encore for the bell-bottoms, thank God.
Satchmo, golden constant, plays in me,

his keen trumpet mocking the motley scene.
Mocking or mourning, not sure which.

"Beautiful"

Your scattered brain blinks on at 2am,
dragging behind it contrails of a dream
fading but heartbreaking in its detail.
You hesitate to call it beautiful

even to yourself—sentimental spam—
but you are rueful switching on the lamp
at the lost connection that's left you all
adrift, a groundlessness, a bubble aswirl

with a jeweled light that bursts at a boy's touch,
leaving a new absence in the air. Much
as you may rub your eyes, random bits still

flicker on, each a pinprick of loss for
something that you never knew was yours,
until it was no longer yours at all.

"Timely Gift"

I know it's true, I'm never going again
to Paris, that time has blinked away, fewer
mind-flights even—but saying so, I'm spun
to when the bunned *frau* in the bakery refused

(purse my lips as I might) to get my French—
ah, one fragrant sweet preened above the others!
Une millefeuille, I intoned, but the witch
(sorry, language, I know, but it's another

heart remembering) stonewalled me, eyes blank.
Millefeuille, une millefeuille!, me, unmanned,
yelling, then a girl rushing in from the back,
offering a smile. *For you*, she says, and hands

me the warm, half- open bag. And that's when
I slowly bow my head, and breathe: in . . . out . . . in . . .

"Lost Poem"

Tragic: the sonnet plunged into the screen
like a skiff into an ocean trench, leaving
not a ruffle in its wake. Or now, unseen,
it sails electronic waves forever weaving

into space, toward alien shores. No excuse:
I knew I'd better save, I fully meant
to save, was just about— But, what's the use
in pounding on my chest in penitence

or crying Why me Lord, why me? Who knows,
maybe it's for the best, an ill-wrought raft
destined to founder, mere rhyme-warped prose,
an old mind's exercise in labored craft.

Still, still. How far might it have taken me,
tall-masted, full-sailed, across the wine-dark sea?

Autobiography of Francesco Fazio, translated by Rose Facchini

Author and Translator

Francesco Thomas Fazio was born in Rome, Italy, on March 29, 1963, to Caitlin MacNamara, the widow of Welsh poet Dylan Thomas, and Giuseppe Fazio, an actor and film director. His arrival was unexpected—his mother was fifty years old, and he was born seven months prematurely. At home, he was affectionately called the "miracle boy." Despite being born to a mother with a history of alcohol addiction, Francesco was perfectly healthy, a fact his family regarded as a gift from God. His birth profoundly strengthened Caitlin's Christian faith.

From an early age, Francesco was immersed in a world of creativity. He watched his mother write diaries, letters, memoirs, and poetry daily, while his father revised film scripts. Their home brimmed with art books, biographies, and screenplays—though notably absent was any trace of mathematics. With his father often away for work, Francesco grew up speaking English with his mother while his Italian remained rudimentary. He attended the International Saint George School in Rome before enrolling in the prestigious San Giuseppe Istituto De Merode in Piazza di Spagna for middle and high school.

Francesco's love for beauty and creativity led him to study architecture at La Sapienza University in Rome, where he excelled for two years. However, life soon presented him with a harrowing choice: to continue his promising academic career or abandon it to help his mother, who was spiraling deeper into alcoholism. Choosing altruism over ambition, Francesco dedicated himself to her care.

The challenge was immense. His father, Giuseppe, had fallen into a state of depression, and Caitlin's three children from her marriage to Dylan Thomas—Llewelyn, Aeron, and Colm—were too distant, both geographically and emotionally, to help. Francesco stood alone in this battle. A long-standing family rift over Francesco's rightful inclusion in an English trust further strained relationships, leaving Caitlin and her youngest son isolated.

Conventional medical treatments for Caitlin's alcoholism yielded little success, and Francesco realized that a return to nature might offer the only hope. Believing that she needed complete immersion in a peaceful, natural environment, free from the temptations of urban life, Francesco moved with Caitlin from Rome to Catania. The diverse landscapes of Sicily—the sea, the volcano, the woods— became their sanctuary. Modernizing his grandparents' villa into a "base camp," Francesco helped his mother reconnect with the natural world. He taught her to swim; she, in turn, taught him acrobatic tap dancing.

Francesco adapted to his new life, becoming a skilled naturalist and trekking guide. He carried pen and paper wherever he went, capturing his memories (as chronicled in *Double Drink Story: My Life with Dylan Thomas*). While exploring Norman castles or mountain trails, he and Caitlin engaged in rich conversations about art, music, and philosophy, weaving together the legacies of Caravaggio, Michelangelo, Giordano Bruno, Rumi, and Mozart. Francesco also studied dance, mastering tango, foxtrot, samba, and cha-cha, which he shared with Caitlin, herself a former student of Isadora Duncan.

Ultimately, it was nature's divine frequency that proved most effective in overcoming Caitlin's struggles with alcohol. Neither Alcoholics Anonymous nor medication like Antabuse could match the restorative power of Sicily's landscapes and the deep connection Francesco fostered with his mother.

Yet Francesco's life was not without tragedy. His villa was ransacked, his brother Colm died under mysterious circumstances, and a ruinous legal battle ensued. Heartbreak followed, and Francesco withdrew from society, retreating to his mother's library to write his own poetry and translate Caitlin's works into Italian.

Now sixty-one, Francesco is piecing together the fragments of his extraordinary life, working to transform them into a film script—a testament to a journey defined by love, resilience, and the search for meaning.

Five Poems from *Risorgere dalle proprie ceneri* | *Rising from Ones's Ashes* **by Francesco Fazio**

"Questo sconosciuto poeta"

Curvo
sul suo consunto menabò
il poeta
è un refuso
un inutile bipede
sputato dal Sistema.

Anima prescelta
nel pizzicare l'arpa divina
vive di stenti
di note fragranti
e crespe illusioni.

Nato forse per errore
destabilizza
creando un'emozione…

Soffice palpito
che frantuma
noi crisalidi
asserragliate
nell'ovattato corbezzolo
del quieto vivere.

"This Unknown Poet"

Bent
over his worn-out scrapbook
the poet
is a misprint
a useless biped
spat out by the System.

Chosen soul
in plucking the divine harp
he lives a life of privations
of scented notes
and creased illusions.

Perhaps born by mistake
he destabilizes
by creating an emotion…

A soft throb
that shatters
us chrysalids
barricaded
in the cocooned arbutus berry
of this insipid living.

"Frequenze in lotta"

Esseri ombra
impalpabili ed invisibili
squarciano la trama
di apparente realtà
derubando il mio me.

L'asse del mio essere
inclinato a trottola
assiste inerme
al furto del mio tempo.

Tentano
con denti di cristallo
di strappar via
la mia anima lattonsola
scrigno di luce e forza vitale
tenacemente aggrappata
a ciò che resta
di bello e pulito
di nostra vita.

La lotta è impari
ma continua spietata.

Posso solo elevarmi
sempre più
mentre mi hanno già afferrato
le caviglie.

"Wrestling Frequencies"

Shadowy beings
impalpable and invisible
tear the weft
of seeming reality
robbing my self.

The axis of my being
tilted like a top
defenseless witnesses
the theft of my time.

They
aim to plunge
their crystal teeth into my newborn soul
casket of light and vital strength
tenaciously clung onto
what remains
of beauty and fairness of life.

The struggle is uneven
but merciless carries on.

I can but only elevate myself
one step further
while they have already
clutched on my ankles.

"Quali dei due mondi?"

Ed io, come Alice
fragile cammino
lungo il velo di cipolla
che separa
il qui ed ora
ricordato dal rintocco
della torre campanaria
ed il novunque
paesino senza tempo e lineamenti.

Invano,
cerco di strappare
la visiera dell'illusione
che affumica i sensi e piega i fatti.

Disorientato,
cerco di scorgere
la bava di indizi
per distinguere
quale dei due mondi è il più vero:

la falsa realtà o la verosimile illusione.

"Which of the Two Worlds?"

And I, like Alice
walk uneasily
along the onion skin
that separates
the here-and-now
recalled by the tolling
of the bell
and the nowhereness
of a hamlet with neither shape nor time.

In vain,
I try to tear off
the veil of illusion
that clouds my senses and bends reality.

Bewildered,
I try to seek
the trail of clues
to ascertain
which of the two worlds is the truest:

the false reality or the likely illusion.

"Alalà"

Distratti
dall'accecante superfluo
non ci accorgiamo
che la silente battaglia continua
in regni a noi ignoti
tra carbonio e silicio.
Il braccio di ferro
in perpetuo dualismo
vede contrapposti
gli assuntori di ossigeno
ed i consumatori di idrogeno.
L'equazione della vita
non è che una scelta
fra il bianco o il nero cavaliere
mentre Aldebaran e la Rubescente Stella
hanno già sceso la visiera.

E tu chi hai scelto?

Il cosmo non conosce il grigio
e rifiuta svilenti compromessi.

"Alalà"

Led astray
by the blinding excess
we don't realize
that the silent battle is ongoing
in realms unknown to us
between carbon and silicon.
The arm-wrestling
in perpetual dualism
sees as their antagonists
the oxygen consumptorēs
and the hydrogen consumers.
The equation of life
is none other than a choice
between the black knight and the white
whilst Aldebaran and the Rubiginous Star
have already lowered their visor.

So whom have you chosen?

The cosmos does not acknowledge gray
and declines indecent compromises.

"Il corpo-tempio"

La cassa armonica dell'udito
ispessita dai trilli petulanti
non è più protesa
ad ascoltare
il rassicurante pulsare del cuore
di Nostra Madre Terra.
La miope vista
rapita e rattrappita
da schermi multicolore
non anela ad incontrare
gli occhi lucenti
delle stelle amiche.
La fucina olfattiva
inebriata di smog
non è più abituata a riconoscere
il sentore sensuale dei fiori
che si profumano per noi.
Le antenne del tatto
ispessite
dall'uso dei tasti
non scorrono più
sulle morbide labbra d'una donna.
Le papille gustative
inselvaggite
non si emozionano più
leccando la salsedine
dal corpo dell'innamorata.

Rischiamo di essere gusci
privi della musica della vita
incapaci di riconoscere
l'autentica vibrazione
di un Amore sincero.

"The Body-Temple"

Our sounding board of hearing
thickened by the nagging shrieks
is no longer outstretched
to listen to
the reassuring heartbeat
of our Mother Earth.
Our myopic sight
enraptured and numbed
by multicolored screens
no longer desires encountering
the luminous eyes
of friendly stars.
Our olfactory forge
inebriated by soot
is no longer accustomed to recognize
the sensual fragrance of flowers
which scent themselves for us.
Our vibrissae of touch
hardened
by the misuse of buttons
no longer run across
the delicate lips of a woman.
Our taste buds
rendered wild
are no longer excited
to taste the saltiness
of our lover's body.

We risk becoming shells
devoid of the music of life
incapable of recognizing
the authentic vibration
of a sincere Love.

Francesco Fazio's Context for "Questo sconosciuto poeta" / "This Unknown Poet"

Poetry, like a broken mirror, reflects the poet's fractured experience. It is spat out by the system, almost indigestible, in a world where contemporary society, alas, prioritizes materialism and possession over being, over divine frequency and vibration. The poet has endured long periods of hardship, surviving at times on nothing more than a single panino, after being stripped of everything: his rights, royalties, land, possessions, talents, and dreams. The phrase "nato forse per errore" (born perhaps by mistake) alludes to his unexpected and premature birth at seven months, when his mother, Caitlin, was fifty. He uses the term "destabilizza" (destabilizes) to evoke the persistent strength of his umbilical connection to the Divine, granting him ability to "see" life from a profoundly different perspective.

Francesco Fazio's Context for "Frequenze in lotta" / "Wrestling Frequencies"

In this poem, the poet seeks to convey the eternal struggle between Good and Evil. He describes the presence of "esseri ombra" ("shadow beings"), reflecting his own experiences of enduring "attacchi psichici esterni" ("external psychic attacks"). As a victim of fiery entities or energetic forces intent on dimming the light of his soul and undermining the strength of his faith, he has faced attempts that force him to resonate at low frequencies, shatter his self-esteem, and sever his profound connection with the Divine.

His solution was to transcend identification with the physical body, choosing instead to view himself as an inhabitant of the body, striving to elevate his spirit toward the Divine. The poet emphasizes that three essential elements—prayer, discipline, and unwavering dedication to his work—enabled him to escape the tunnel of despair and reclaim his spiritual harmony.

Francesco Fazio's Context for "Quali dei due mondi" / "Which of the Two Worlds?"

The poem reflects on the illusory nature of perception, drawing a clear allusion to *Alice in Wonderland*. Like Alice, who is thrust into a surreal world where the line between the real and the imaginary blurs, the poet explores the fragility of reality. This exploration is deeply autobiographical, shaped by a series of negative experiences: the death of his brother Colm, the son of Dylan Thomas; a failed lawsuit; and the loss of the love of his life. These events have distorted the contours of reality in the poet's perception of his life.

In search of solace and spiritual clarity, the author often walked along an ancient path near the church of Sant'Andrea in the Baracche district (Capo Mulini - Acireale). This path, leading to a water mill, offered a space for meditation and renewal of the soul. The location itself feels like a portal through time, a fairy-tale dimension where space and time intertwine in a dreamlike harmony.

Francesco Fazio's Context for "Alalà"

The author, captivated by the works of Philip Corso, Frank Scully, Linda Moulton Howe, Roberto Pinotti, and Alfredo Lissoni, and an admirer of the Sicilian *contattista* Eugenio Siragusa, believes that the seemingly invisible is teeming with presences. Life, he contends, is distributed across all directions of the cosmos, and in its immeasurable vastness, it is unreasonable to consider humanity the only chosen beings. He fondly recalls visiting Mount Manfrè and Mount Sona on Mount Etna with his mother, Caitlin, in search of glimpses "beyond," hoping to observe the highways of the heavens. This quest for understanding and connection with the universe is deeply entwined with the poem's theme of dualism: the inevitable choice between aligning with or against the forces of Good. The poem concludes with a profound existential question: "E tu chi hai scelto?" ("So, whom have you chosen?"). This fundamental choice, the author suggests, shapes both our karma and our destiny.

Francesco Fazio's Context for "Il corpo-tempio" / "The Body-Temple"

This poem stems from the poet's observations of younger generations, whose values, ethics, and goals, he believes, differ profoundly from those of his own at sixty years old. The text invites reflection on the overwhelming demands of modern society and humanity's growing disconnection from the harmony of planet Earth.

The poet reflects on a time when the human mind's frequency was in harmony with the heartbeat of the Earth—the Schumann resonance at 7.83 hertz. He laments that this once-possibly synchronized dance between humanity and the planet has fallen out of step. In developed countries, people are increasingly shielded by electronic devices, distracted from the natural world, and at risk of dulling their primary channels of perception—the five senses. In the relentless pursuit of an illusory and empty existence, the poet warns, humanity risks severing its connection to the profound truths that surround and sustain us.

Context Paragraphs and Biographies

Context (Anne van den Dool, Guillaume van der Graft, Ted van Lieshout, and Arno Bohlmeijer)

These three poems seamlessly blend boldness and vulnerability, humor and poignancy, lightness and depth. They stand out for their unusual frankness and original perspectives, particularly in their exploration of children. When acclaimed poets tackle the theme of children—whether examining the process of growing up, the timeless essence of childhood, or the child within us—they create works of exceptional strength and resonance. Even when faced with challenging or humorous translation choices (like deciding between "kiss" or "snog"), the poets approached the task with enthusiasm and collaboration.

Author

Anne van den Dool, at just thirty-two years old, is one of Holland's most accomplished young authors, celebrated for her prose, poetry, and cultural journalism. She also collaborates with prestigious institutions like the National Theater, Museum, and Library.

Author

Guillaume van der Graft (Willem Barnard) authored around 2,000 poems, earning half a dozen awards. In addition to his literary accomplishments, he was a theologian who wrote lyrics for church hymnals. During World War II, he was transported to Berlin, where he published work in the illegal journal *Parade der Profeten.*

Author

Ted van Lieshout is a true international phenomenon, excelling as a poet, novelist, artist, screenwriter, and lyricist. To date, he has published ninety books and won seventeen major awards. His work is renowned for its remarkable variety in themes and styles, ranging from utterly playful to deeply serious—or often both at once, blending humor with profound insight.

Translator
Arno Bohlmeijer is a queer poet and novelist, and a recipient of the 2021 PEN America grant. His work has been published in six countries and featured in over two dozen esteemed journals and reviews between 2019 and 2025. He is included in *Universal Oneness: An Anthology of Magnum Opus Poems from Around the World* (2019), and his upcoming novel, *Narrowly*—a story about unusual empathy—is set to be released in September 2025.

ENGLISH

Context (Yuan Changming)

In recent years, I've been writing extensively in a self-created subgenre I call "bilingual-cultural poems," aiming to foster linguistic and cultural exchange through poetry. To my delight, this form has resonated with many readers and editors. In 2022, I published a full-length collection titled *Sinosaur: Bilingual-Cultural Poems* (https://redhawkpublications.com/Sinosuar-p504579309). Since then, I've continued to explore this form, though more sporadically. "Lesson 12" is one such casual experiment.

Author
Yuan Changming co-edits *Poetry Pacific* with Allen Yuan. His accolades include sixteen chapbooks, fourteen Pushcart Prize nominations, and appearances in *Best of the Best Canadian Poetry* (2008–2017), *BestNewPoemsOnline*, and 2,109 other publications across fifty-one countries. In 2022, Yuan expanded into fiction writing and publishing, debuting his hybrid novel *Detaching*, now available on Amazon. While his forthcoming duology, *Mabakoola: Paradise Regained*, is set to be released by Running Wild Press in early 2026, his "silver romance" *The Tuner* and short story collection *Flashbacks* have just been released.

Context (James Croal Jackson)

Whenever my family gathers—fifteen years after my father's passing—we inevitably talk about cleaning out his personal space in the basement, still filled with so many of the items that meant so much to him. Yet, we never quite get around to it. And when we finally do, what then?

Author

James Croal Jackson, a Filipino-American poet and film production professional, is the author of the chapbooks *A God You Believed In* (Pinhole Poetry, 2023) and *Count Seeds with Me* (Ethel Zine & Micro-Press, 2022). His recent work appeared in *Ghost City Review, Little Patuxent Review,* and *Lamplit Underground.* Based in Pittsburgh, Pennsylvania, he edits *The Mantle Poetry.* Discover more of his work at jamescroaljackson.com

Context (David Dephy)

The image of the waving silk is a clue in itself. The poem "The Waving Silk" begins and ends with sounds and visions carried by a particular linguistic stream, symbolizing longing and premonition. In this piece, the spirit of the work is intricately entwined with its form of expression. The poem is about the poet's mother, whom he lost on February 14, 2023. It is one of two poems he wrote in her memory. She owned a soft, magical, and masterfully crafted silk scarf that the poet had adored since childhood, always believing that the spirit of mysteries dwelled within its gentle waves.

Author

David Dephy is an award-winning American poet, novelist, essayist, and multi-media artist with a Master of Fine Arts degree accredited by Globe Language USA. He is the founder of Poetry Orchestra and American Poetry Intersection, as well as the Poet-in-Residence for Brownstone Poets for 2024-2025. His poem, "A Sense of Purpose," has been sent to the Moon in 2025 as part of a collaboration between The Lunar Codex, NASA, and Brick Street Poetry. Recognized as a "Literature Luminary" by Bowery Poetry, a "Stellar Poet" by Voices of Poetry, and an "Incomparable Poet" by Statorec, he has also been called "Brilliant Grace" by Headline Poetry & Press and praised for his "Extremely Unique Poetic Voice" by Cultural Daily. In 2017,

Dephy was exiled from his native country of Georgia, where he was granted immediate and indefinite political asylum in the U.S. His wife and 9-year-old son joined him in the U.S. in 2023, after seven years of exile. He currently lives and works in New York City.

Context (Luke Dylan Ramsey)
A professor in my MFA program stated in class that love poetry is dead. While I understand the perspective behind this claim, I (respectfully) disagree. However, this particular poem is not exactly a love poem—it's more of a breakup poem. I was in a long-term relationship where we both knew it had an expiration date, but neither of us wanted to see it end. This poem captures my feelings about the eventual dissolution of that relationship, its aftermath, and how it impacted other parts of my life, including my dream life.

Author
Luke Dylan Ramsey (he/they) is a poet, fiction writer, screenwriter, visual artist, lay academic, head editor of *Just Keep Up Magazine*, and co-host of the podcast *Mapping the Zone*.

FRENCH

Context (Laura Hess)
Due to her experiences and the associations formed in her mind with the language with which she grew up, Laura Hess realized that when she learned French in college, she was able to access thought processes she hadn't been able to access in English. A different language allowed her mind to enter new imaginative realms. The poetry she writes in French offers a means of transcending limitations, while translating her own poems into English presents a unique challenge. She marvels at the process of translation, wondering how it can bring the essence of the original work into a new form.

Author and Translator
Laura Hess lives in Texas where she teaches eleventh-grade English

at a classical curriculum charter school. She has been doing yoga and acrobatics since the age of seven and, after many years, still enjoys doing cartwheels and viewing the upside-down world while standing on her hands or head whenever possible.

Context (Henri Meschonnic, Gaby Bedetti, and Don Boes)

In our attempt to animate the poems, we resisted smoothing the poetic line or imposing lyricism where it doesn't exist. Meschonnic's approach challenges the predominantly lyrical and autobiographical current of contemporary American poetry. His poems resist particularizing nouns and verbs, as broader terms often enhance the expansiveness of his brief compositions. The irregular lines, sparse vocabulary, unexpected enjambments, and reliance on the most colloquial verbs, nouns, prepositions, pronouns, and syntax all serve to map voices rather than create poems in the conventional sense. Meschonnic employs a universal, simplified vocabulary to capture the rhythm of language, the breath, and the line, achieving an almost diaphanous effect.

Author

Henri Meschonnic (1932–2009) is a key figure in French "new poetics," internationally recognized for his translations of the Old Testament and his *Critique du rythme: Anthropologie historique du langage*. His numerous poetry awards include the Max Jacob International Poetry Prize, the Mallarmé Prize, the Jean Arp Francophone Literature Prize, the Guillevic-Ville de Saint-Malo Grand Prize for Poetry, and the title of Chevalier de L'Ordre des Arts et des Lettres.

Translators

Gabriella Bedetti's translations of Meschonnic's essays have been published in *New Literary History* and *Critical Inquiry*. She also interviewed him for *Diacritics* and has written about his work in *New Literary History*

Don Boes's poems combine intricate wordplay with deadpan

seriousness. He is the author of three books: *Good Luck with That* (FutureCycle Press), *Railroad Crossing* (Finishing Line Press), and *The Eighth Continent* (Northeastern University Press). *The Eighth Continent* was selected by award-winning poet A. R. Ammons to receive the Samuel French Morse Poetry Prize.

Context (Mirko Boncaldo)

Selected from *Senza titoli. Sovversi (Subverses)* published by Transeuropa in 2022, this is electric poetry, crackling like the chatter of teeth. Sensitivity and sentimentality are banned from Boncaldo's poetry: no "mere fact" is exhausted in a description. Here, the language plays a game against itself, testing its limits to reveal the unlimited, or, if we prefer, the irreducibility of being within the content of a proposition. A climax of indomitable verses rises from rarefied atmospheres, even ironic at times, thickening the expressiveness in a drift that shatters the ego, the word, until all referents are lost.

Author and Translator

Mirko Boncaldo was born in the same town as Emilio Isgrò, remains perpetually twenty-five years old, lives in Bologna, organizes trips to the future, and takes an interest in gender and environmental issues. He is the author of *Subverses* (2025)—published in French by Le Lys Bleu—and *Senza Titoli. Sovversi* (2022), published in Italian by Transeuropa, which was a finalist for the International Nabokov Prize and Lorenzo Montano Prize. He has also completed *Senzanome (Nameless)*, which he is co-translating with the poet and translator Ranald Barnicot (1948), and which is a finalist for the International Prize Fondazione Amedeo Modigliani. His verses have been published in anthologies and literary magazines such as *Italian Poetry Review, Il Segnale, Frequenze Poetiche, Articoli Liberi, CedroMag,* and on digital literary magazines and blogs, *L'Estroverso, Carte Sensibili, Distruttori di Terre, Radura Poetica, L'Incendiario Poesia Ultracontemporanea, Versante Ripido, Recours au poème,*

Neutopia, *Zibaldoni e altre meraviglie*, *L'Equivoco*, *Hook Literary Magazine*, and more. His poems have been translated in French, English, Spanish, and Russian.

Context (Antonio Spagnuolo and Ivano Mugnaini)

In his dense, concentrated poems, Antonio Spagnuolo expresses himself through a series of variations on a central theme, which ultimately returns to an identical root: mourning and grief for the loss of his beloved life partner. His personal sorrow organically transforms into a universal grief, one that encompasses the regrets and wounds of all, soothed only by memory and writing.

Author

Antonio Spagnuolo was born in Naples on July 21, 1931. He founded and directed the magazines *Prospettive Culturali* and *Iride*. He also established and directed the book series *L'assedio della poesia*, which published prominent authors of national renown, such as Gilberto Finzi, Gio Ferri, Giorgio Bàrberi Squarotti, Massimo Pamio, Ettore Bonessio di Terzet, Giuliano Manacorda, Alberto Cappi, Dante Maffia, and others. Spagnuolo has participated in numerous national and international visual poetry exhibitions and is featured in many anthologies. He contributes to various periodicals and magazines across different cultural spheres. Currently, he directs the book series *Frontiere della poesia contemporanea* for the publisher La valle del tempo.

Translator

Ivano Mugnaini graduated from the University of Pisa. He is a consultant, editor, and translator. On his website, www. ivanomugnaini.it, he publishes works by both classical and contemporary authors. From 2000 to 2012, he edited the *Panorami Congeniali* column on the Bompiani RCS website. He also edits the *Quaderni Dedalus*, yearbooks of contemporary fiction, and serves on the jury of several literary prizes. Mugnaini has published the short story collections *La casa gialla* and *L'algebra della vita*, as well as the poetry books *Controtempo*, *Inadeguato all'eterno*, and *Il tempo* *salvato*. His recent works include the novel *Lo specchio di Leonardo* and the poetry collection *La creta indocile*. He also edits the literary blog *DEDALUS* at www.ivanomugnainidedalus.wordpress.com.

Context (Adriano Espínola and Charles Perrone)

The three poems in this cluster address the Portuguese language itself, a foundational tongue in European lyric; the critical issue of the Amazon's survival, a global concern; and a significant anniversary with which elders everywhere can relate. The challenges of translation involve capturing references to phenomena specific to the Portuguese-speaking world, preserving rhyme schemes, and conveying the idiosyncratic rhythms of the original.

Author

Adriano Espínola is an active poet and retired Professor of Brazilian Literature. Born and raised in Fortaleza, the capital of the Northeastern state of Ceará, he moved to Rio de Janeiro in the late 1980s, where he later became a member of the city's Academy of Letters. Over the decades, he has published numerous critically acclaimed works of poetry and criticism, including *Táxi ou poema de amor passageiro*, which was translated into English as *Taxi or Poem of Love in Transit*.

Translator

Charles A. Perrone is Professor Emeritus of Portuguese and Luso-Brazilian Culture and Literature at the University of Florida. He is the author of several influential books on Brazilian song and poetry, including *Seven Faces: Brazilian Poetry since Modernism* (1997) and *Brazil, Lyric, and the Americas* (2010). A translator of lyric poetry and fiction since the 1980s, Perrone's own poetry can be found at moriapoetry.com. He currently resides in Santa Cruz, California, nestled between the seaside and the redwoods.

Context (Alberto Marcos)

"When on the move, in transit, sometimes we inhabit in words or words inhabit in us. In the dissociation between what we see and what we look at, we believe we can find a clearer image of ourselves. The outside becomes a landscape of memories where we keep looking for who we are, who we were or who we believe we could be." This is an excerpt of the author's new poetry collection, inspired by his move from Spain to England and his travels back and forth between site visits and school runs.

Author

Alberto Marcos is an architect and designer born in Madrid. He founded Amps Arquitectura y Diseño in 2006. (www.amps.es). He is the author of several poetry books: *Mujer desnudando el Mediterráneo* (Calambur, 1999_first prize UPM poetry award), *MAYA* (Pez Privé, 2001), and *NSEO, la urdimbre del mapa* (Inconstant, 2014). He divides his time between Madrid and Hampshire.

Translator

Sacha Bancroft Cooke, a modern languages graduate from the University of Cambridge, has worked as a freelance translator for over 20 years. She runs the educational consultancy ninetonineworld (www.ninetonineworld.com) and a summer camp for girls in the UK (www.countryhousecamp.com).

Context (Jorge Armando Ríos and Ivy Raff)

The author of the Spanish version and I collaborated on the translation of *It's More Likely*. The natural rhythm of Spanish suggests stanza and line breaks, which were absent in the initial English translation (which, like the original, had no stanza breaks). Inserting stanza breaks changes the visual experience for the reader, making it different from the original poem, but it better preserves its pauses, rhythms, and tone.

Author

Jorge Rios is a human rights attorney and multi-genre writer from Monterrey, Mexico. His debut novel, *Viento del oeste*, is forthcoming from the Autonomous University of Nuevo Leon Press in summer 2025. His poems and short stories appear in *Luvina Magazine, Libros de la Politica*, and the *Ministry of Mexican Culture Anthology*. Jorge's work has earned him the FONCA Young Creators Fellowship and a residency at Under the Volcano, where he currently serves as Director of Operations.

Translator

Ivy Raff is the author of *What Remains* (Editorial DALYA, forthcoming 2025), a bilingual English/Spanish poetry collection that won the Alberola International Poetry Prize, and *Rooted and Reduced to Dust* (Finishing Line Press, 2024). Her *Best of the Net*-nominated poems and translations have appeared in *Ninth Letter, Hayden's Ferry Review, Electric Literature*, and *West Trade Review*, among numerous others, as well as in the anthologies *London Independent Story Prize Anthology* (LISP, 2023), and *Aesthetica Creative Writing Prize Annual* (Aesthetica, 2023). Ivy serves artist communities as MacDowell's Senior Systems Project Manager and as a member of *Seventh Wave Magazine's* editorial team

www.ingramcontent.com/pod-product-compliance
Lightning Source LLC
Chambersburg PA
CBHW050014090426
42734CB00020B/3268